MW01463309

# This Book Belong To

..............................................................................

# Color Test Page

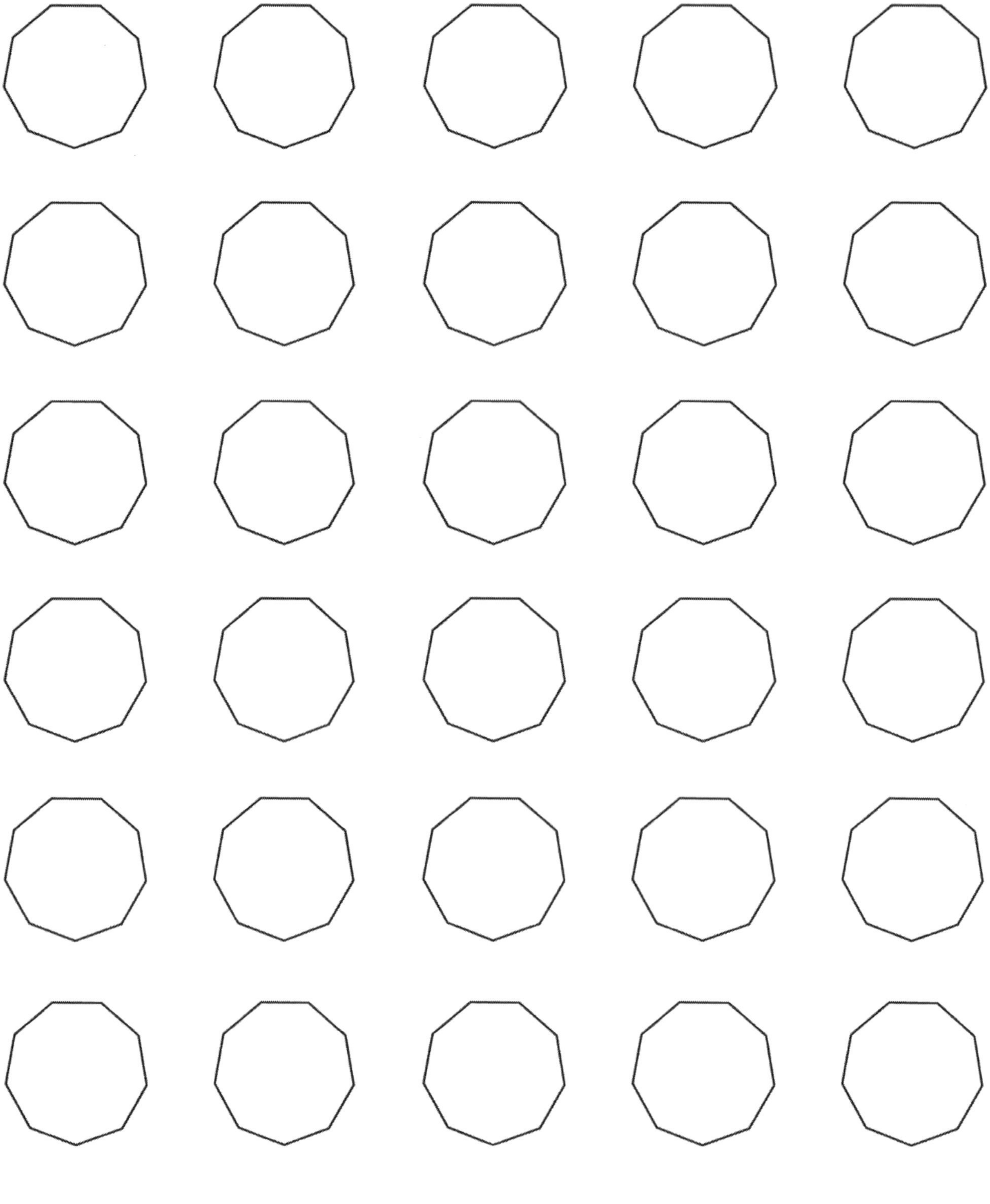

COOL

COOL

COOL

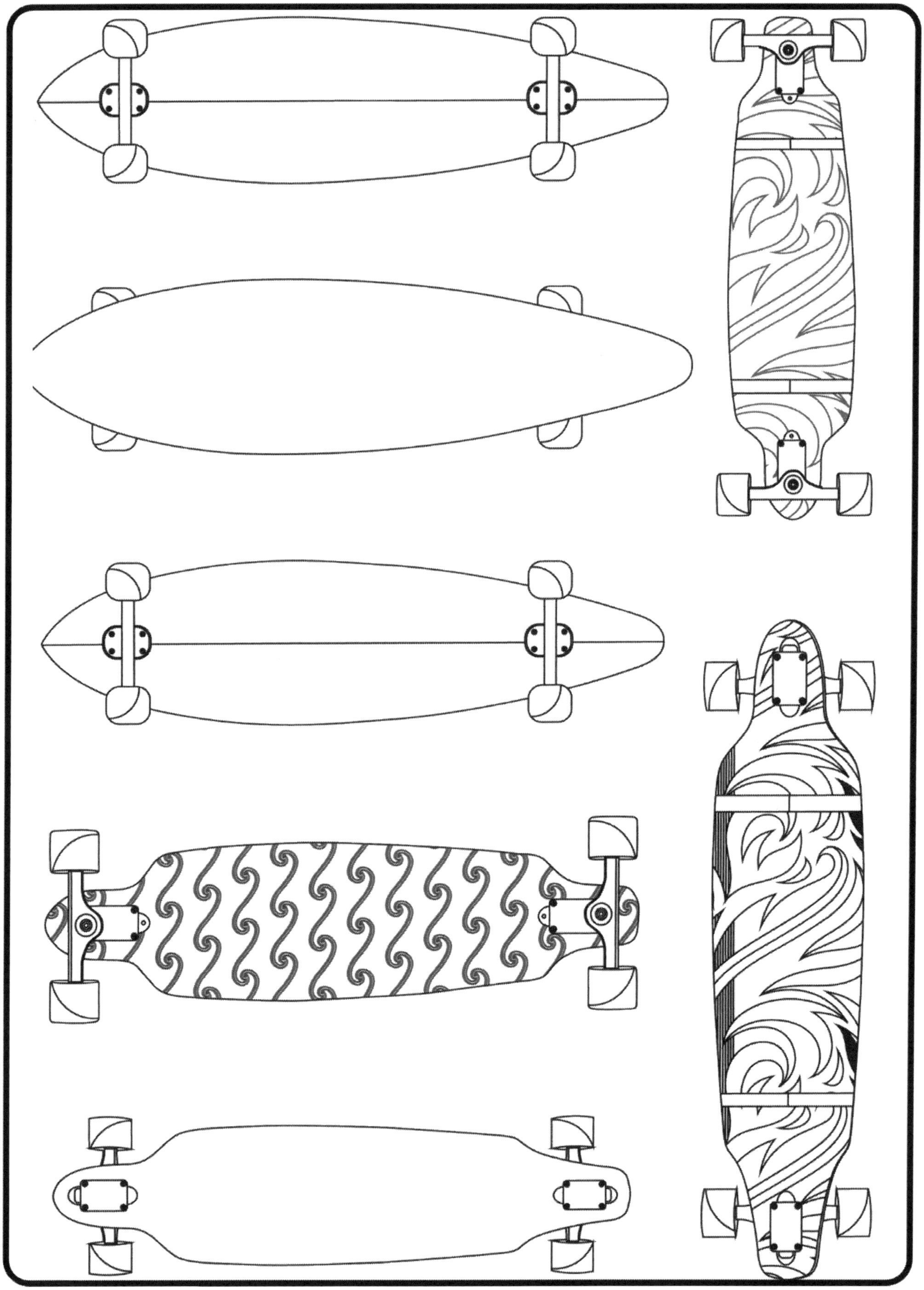

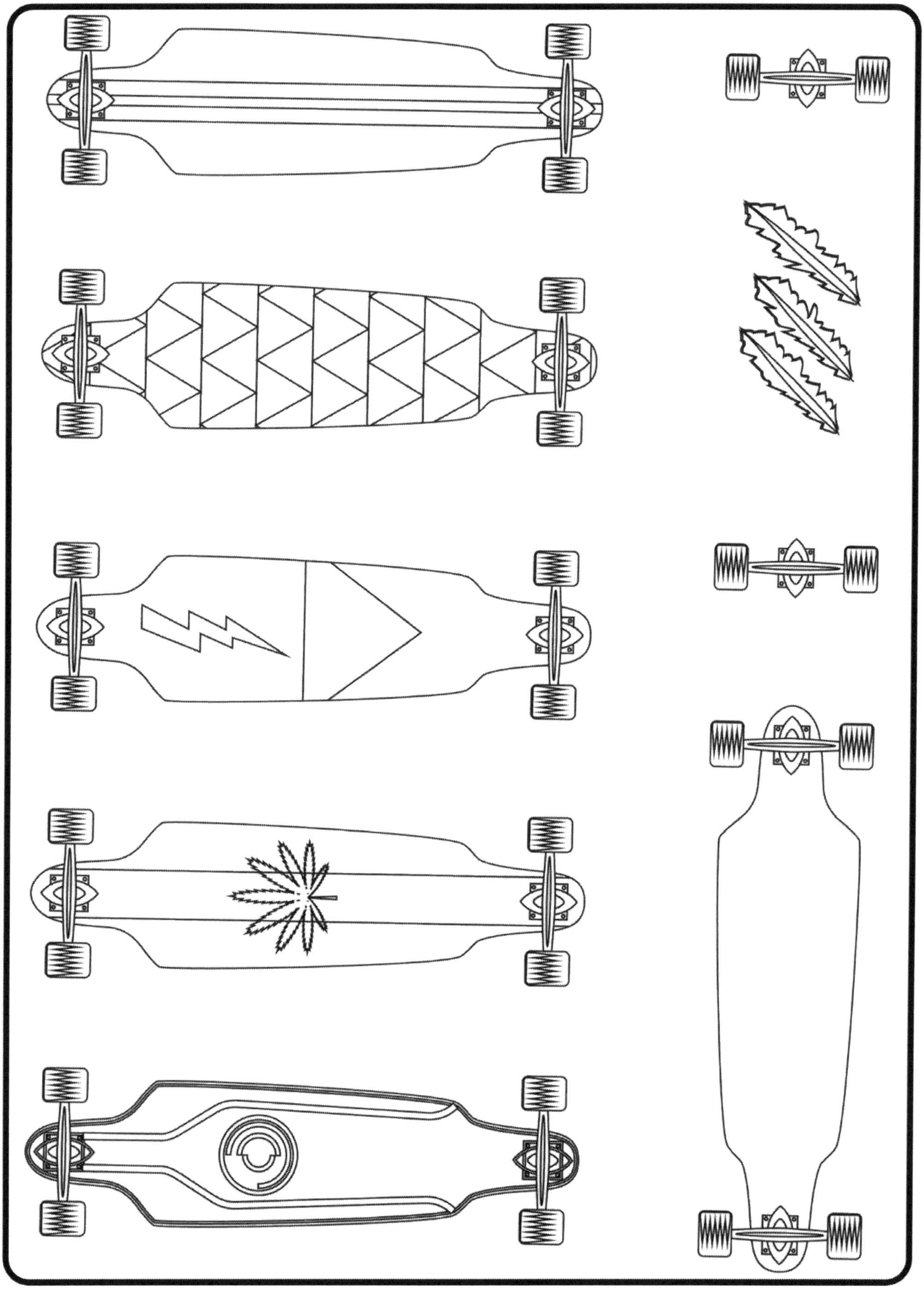

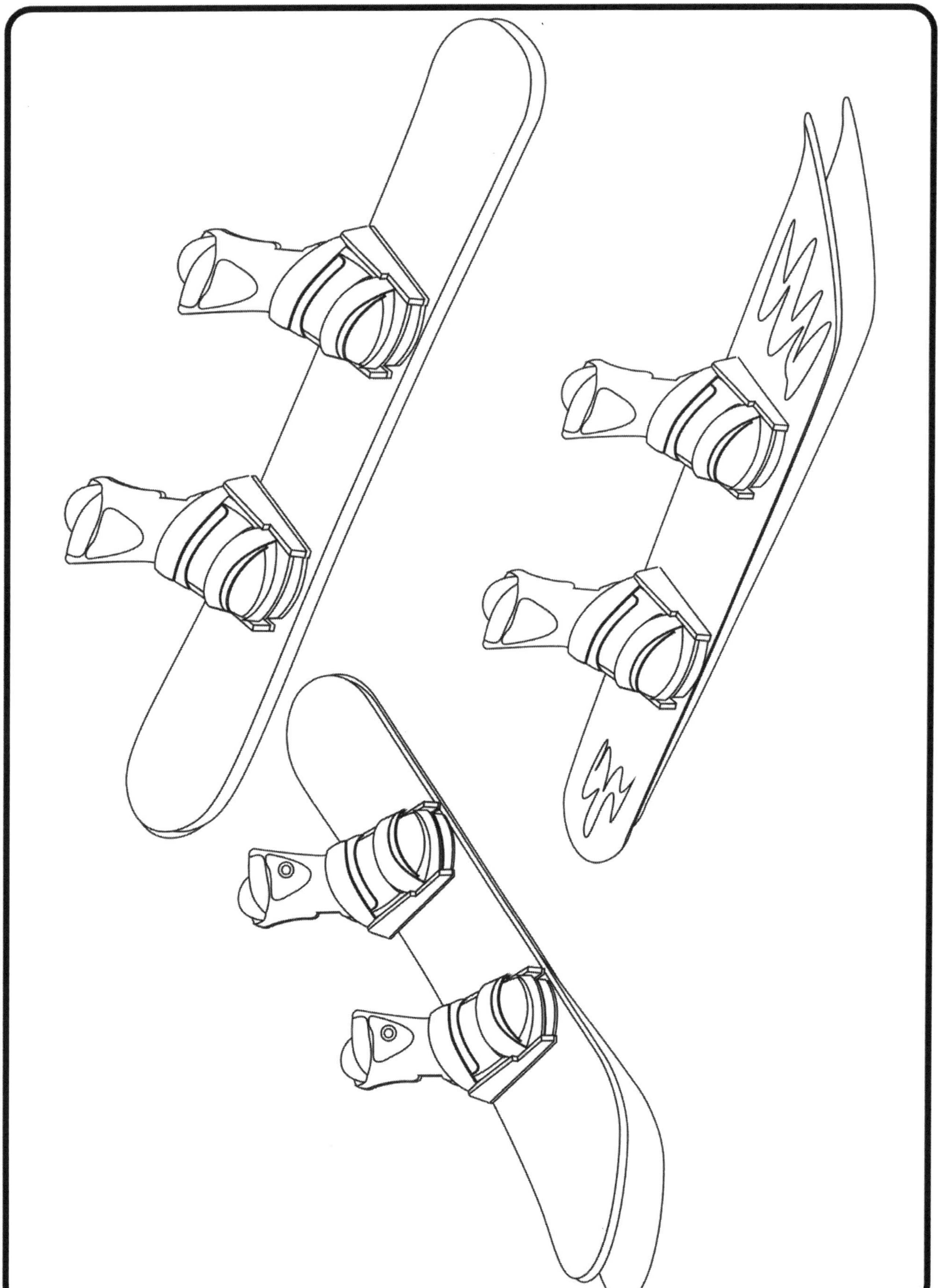

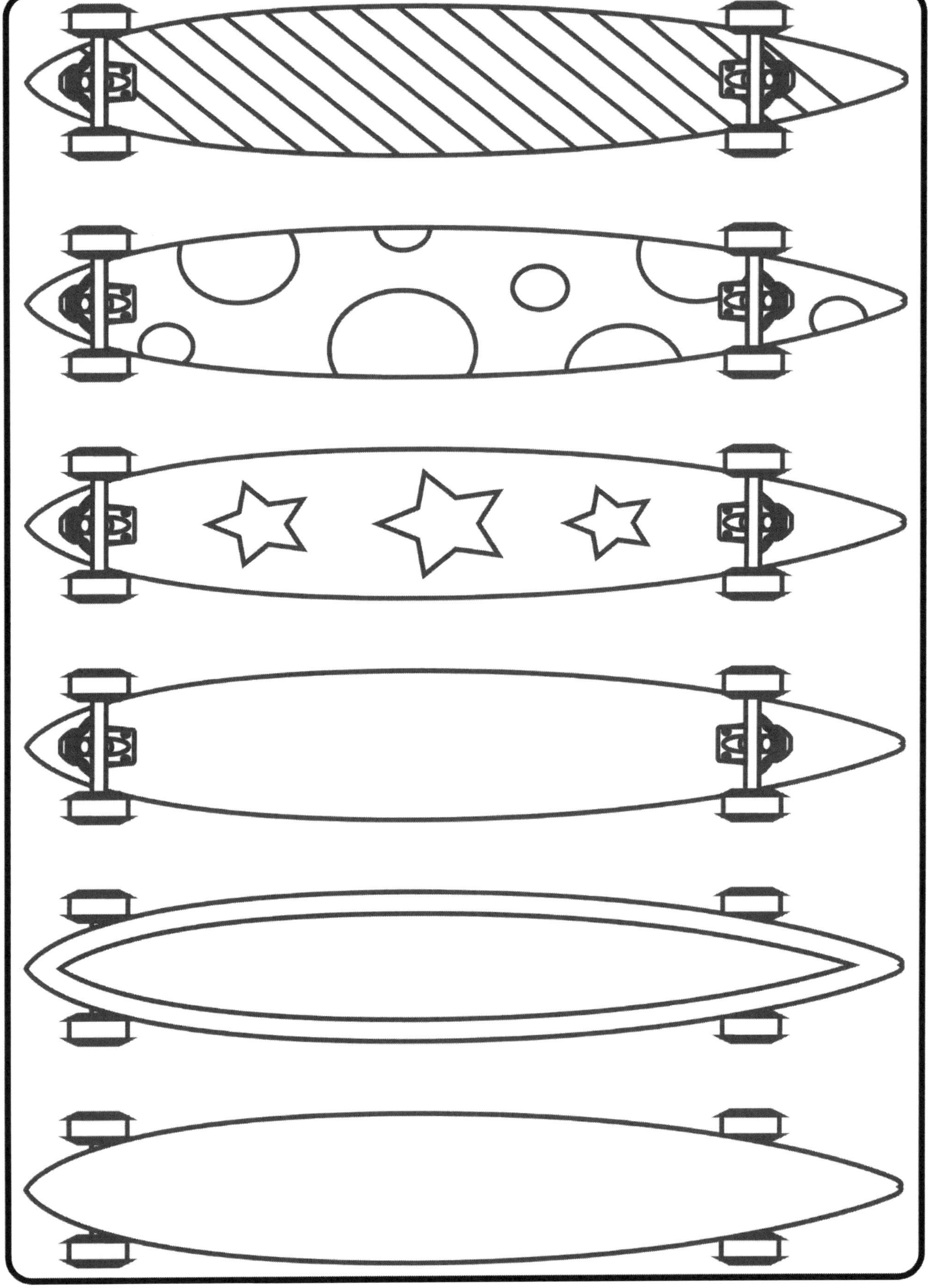

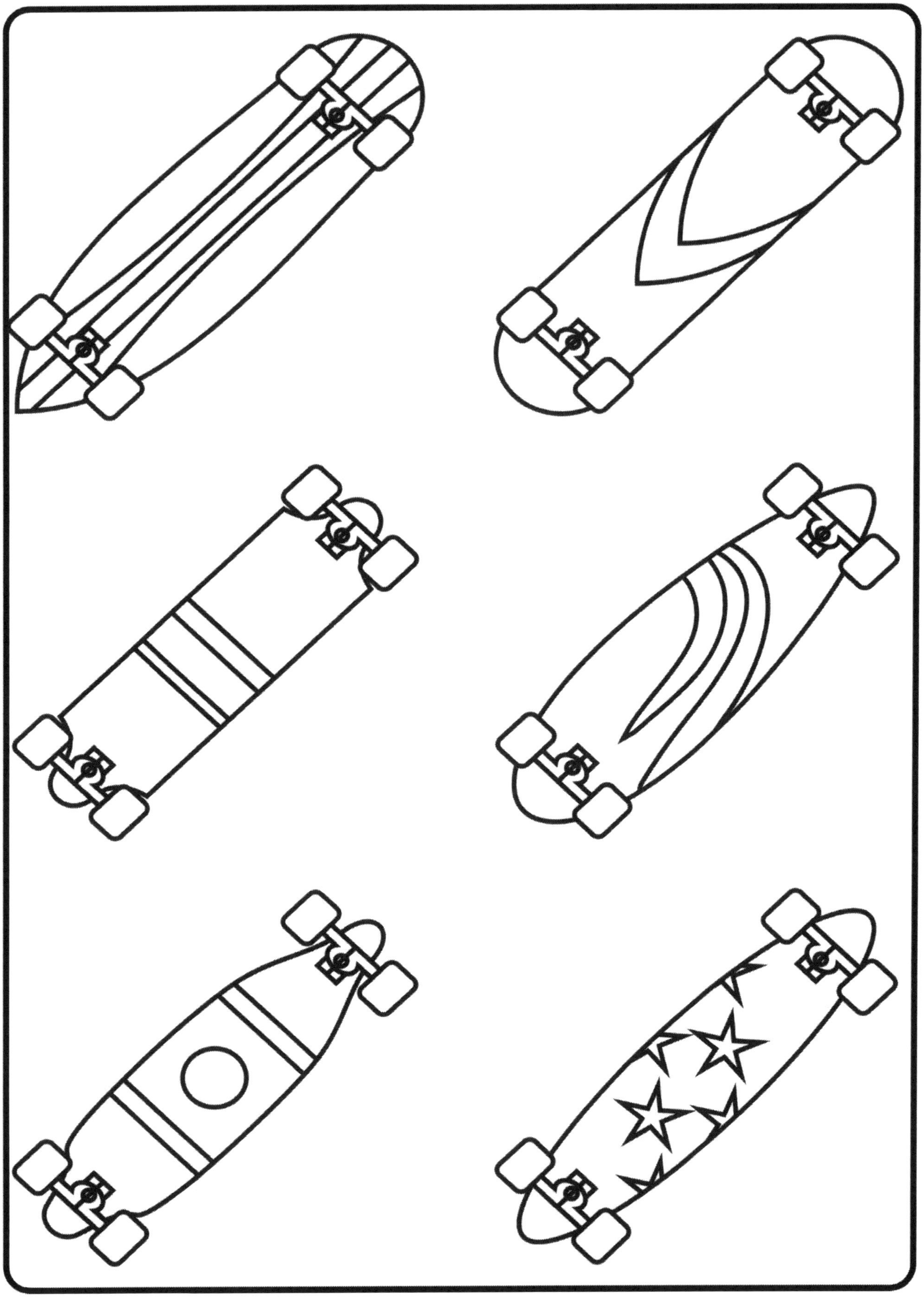

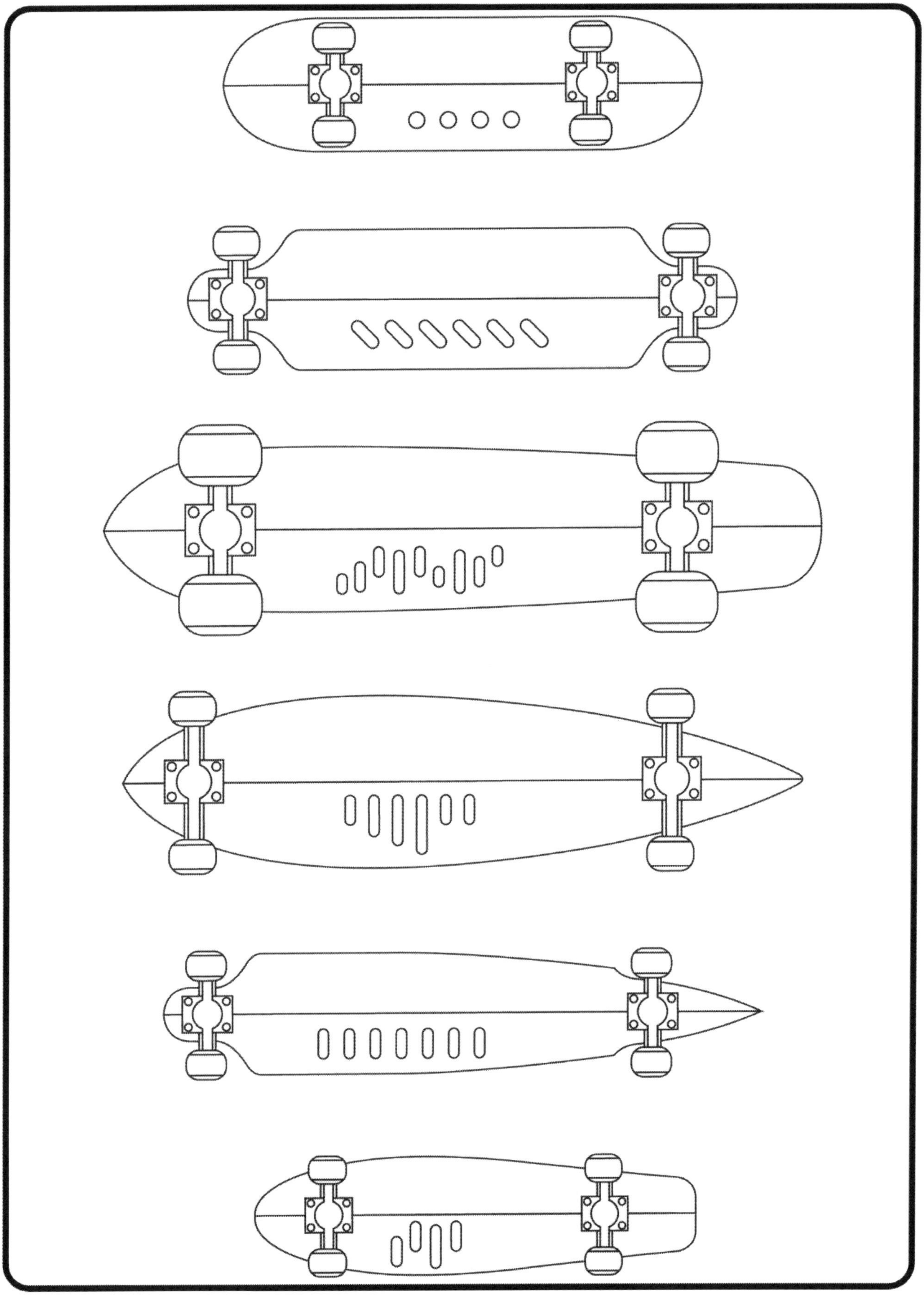

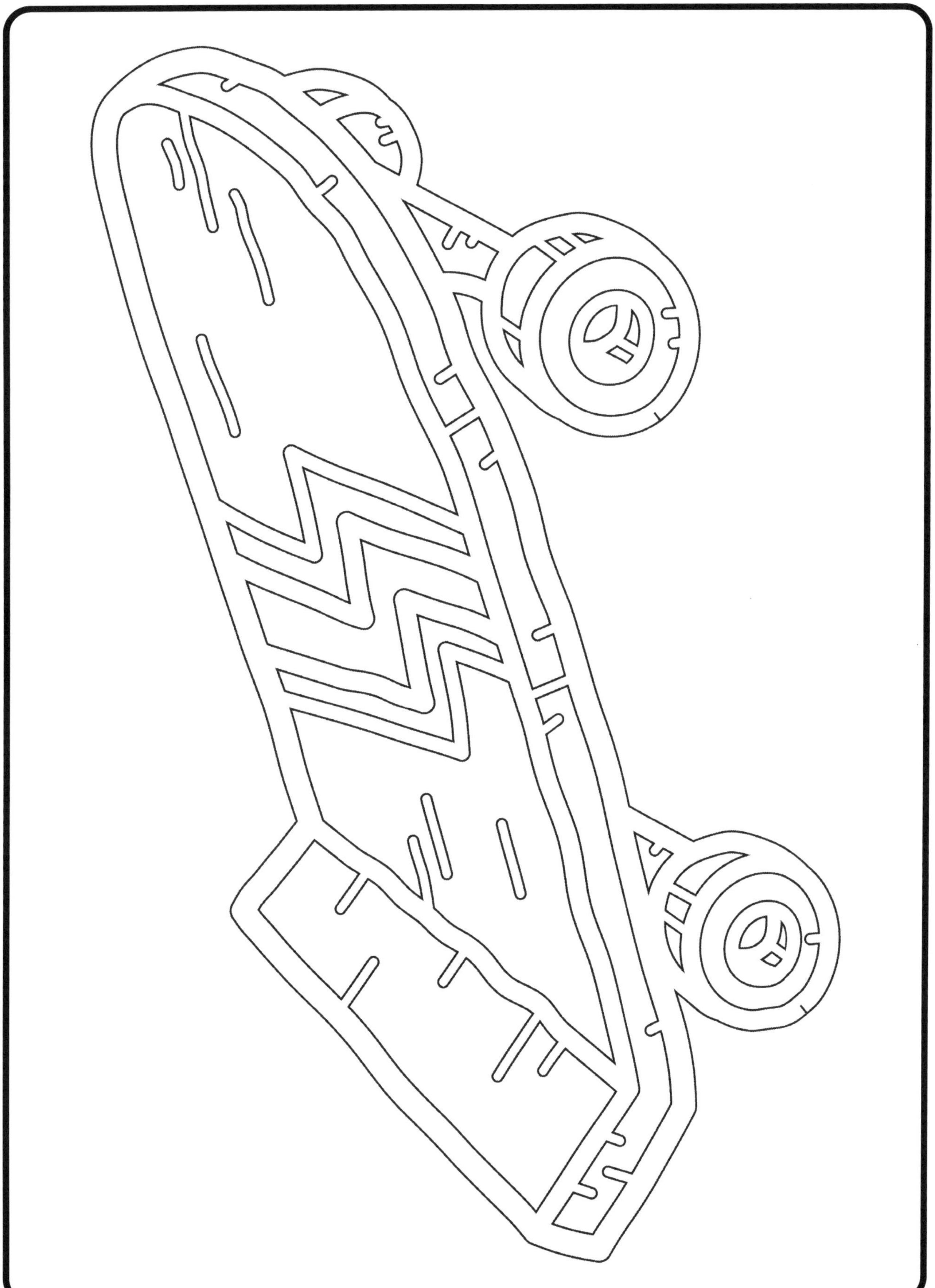

Made in the USA
Middletown, DE
20 March 2024

51784658R00051